THE STATES AND THEIR SYMBOLS

Wisconsin

Facts and Symbols

by Emily McAuliffe

Consultant:
Gerilyn Schneider
Capitol Tours and Information
Wisconsin Department of Administration

Hilltop Books
an imprint of Franklin Watts
A Division of Grolier Publishing
New York   London   Hong Kong   Sydney
Danbury, Connecticut

Hilltop Books
http://publishing.grolier.com

Library of Congress Cataloging-in-Publication Data
McAuliffe, Emily.
  Wisconsin facts and symbols/by Emily McAuliffe.
     p. cm.—(The states and their symbols)
  Includes bibliographical references and index.
  Summary: Presents information about the state of Wisconsin, its nickname, motto,
  and emblems.
  ISBN 0-7368-0217-7
  1. Emblems, State—Wisconsin—Juvenile literature. [1. Emblems, State—Wisconsin.
2. Wisconsin.] I. Title. II. Series: McAuliffe, Emily. States and their symbols.
CR203.W6M38 1999
977.5—dc21
                                                                    98-41527
                                                                         CIP
                                                                          AC

Editorial Credits
Christy Steele, editor; Steve Christensen, cover designer; Linda Clavel, illustrator;
   Kimberly Danger and Sheri Gosewisch, photo researchers

Photo Credits
A.B. Sheldon, 22 (top)
Kent and Donna Dannen, 18
Life Through the Lens/Kim Karpeles, 22
Lynn M. Stone, cover, 20
Marijo Erzinger, 22
Mark Schneider, 6
One Mile Up, Inc., 8, 10 (inset)
Root Resources/Ruth A. Smith, 14
Terry Donnelly, 10, 16
Visuals Unlimited/Steve Maslowski, 12

Table of Contents

Lake Superior

Lake Superior

Michigan

WISCONSIN

Wisconsin River

Minnesota

Mississippi River

Green Bay ○
Lambeau Field and
Packer Hall of Fame

Perrot State Park 🏛

Lake Michigan

Madison ★   Milwaukee ○

Old World Wisconsin 🏛

Iowa

Illinois

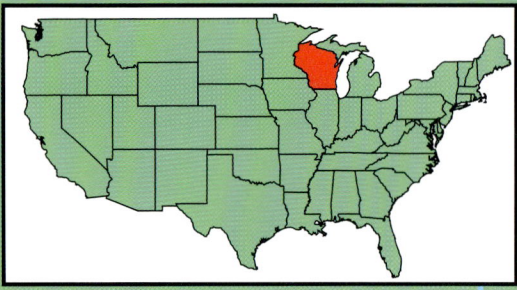

Legend:
- ✪ Capital
- ○ City
- 🏛 Places to Visit
- 〜 River

Fast Facts

Capital City: Madison is Wisconsin's capital city.

Largest City: Milwaukee is Wisconsin's largest city. More than 600,000 people live in Milwaukee.

Size: Wisconsin is the 23rd-largest state. It covers 65,499 square miles (169,642 square kilometers).

Location: Wisconsin is in the midwestern United States.

Population: 5,169,677 people live in Wisconsin (U.S. Census Bureau, 1997 estimate).

Statehood: Wisconsin became the 30th state on May 29, 1848.

Natural Resources: Wisconsin has stone, lead, sand, and limestone.

Manufactured Goods: Factory workers in Wisconsin make paper products and medical equipment.

Crops: Wisconsin farmers are the leading producers of corn and snap beans. Farmers also grow potatoes, soybeans, and cranberries. Cows in Wisconsin produce milk. Workers make cheese from the milk.

State Name and Nickname

Most people believe that Wisconsin is named after its largest river. French explorer Louis Jolliet named the river "Miskonsing." The spelling of the river's name changed several times. By 1800, Ouisconsin was the river's name.

No one knows what the word Wisconsin means. Some people believe it comes from a Native American word. The state name may come from an Ojibwe word that means "gathering of the waters." Or it may come from a Chippewa word that means "grassy place."

Wisconsin's nickname is the Badger State. The nickname comes from early lead miners. They lived in mines or dug holes in Wisconsin's hills. The holes reminded people of badgers' dens. Today, some University of Wisconsin sports teams are called the Badgers.

In 1674, Louis Jolliet became the first European to discover the Wisconsin River.

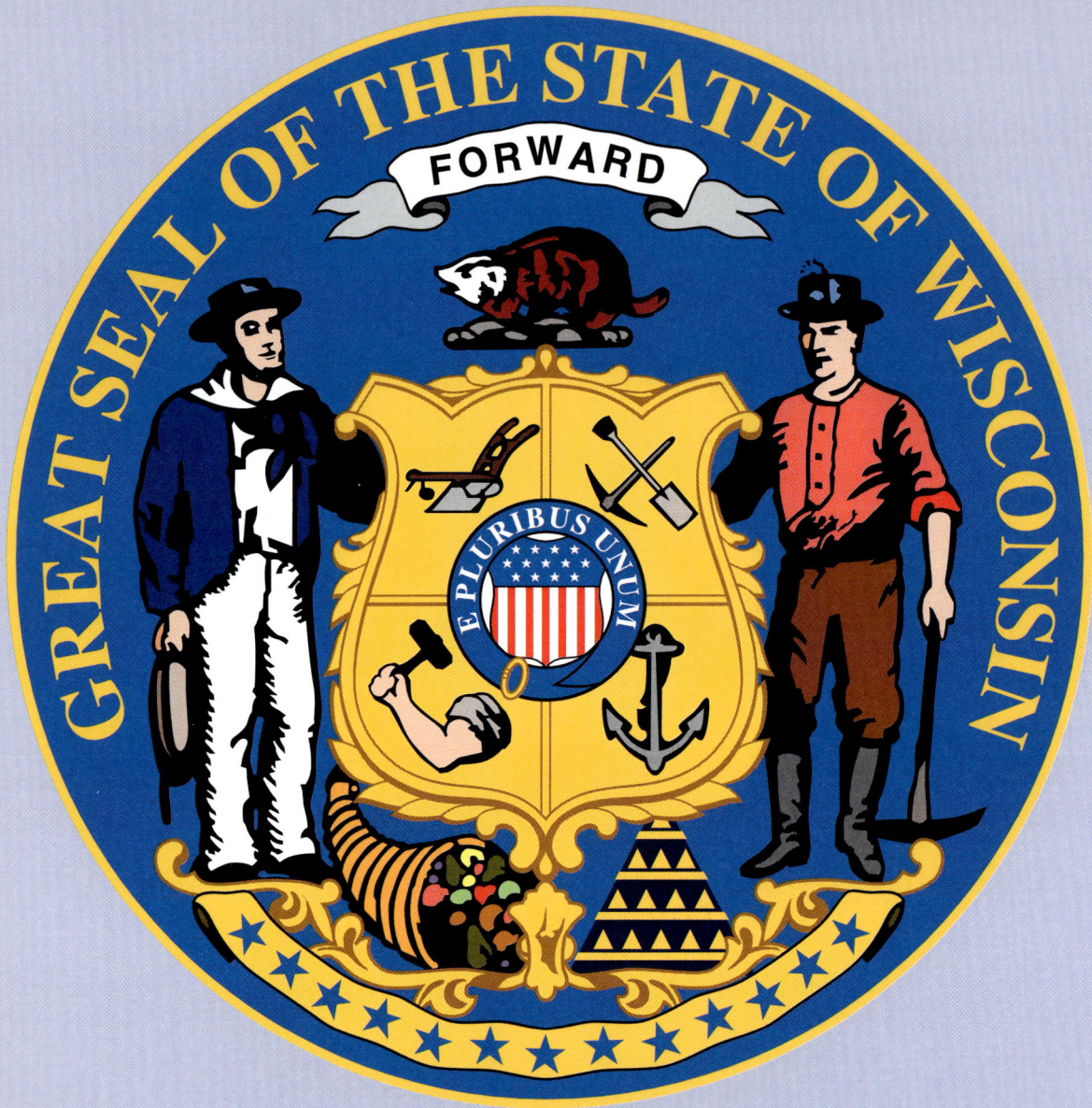

GREAT SEAL OF THE STATE OF WISCONSIN

FORWARD

E PLURIBUS UNUM

State Seal and Motto

Wisconsin has had two official seals. A seal reminds Wisconsinites of their state government. The seal also makes government papers official.

Lawmakers used the territorial seal before Wisconsin joined the United States. Government officials chose the current state seal in 1848. Wisconsin became a state that year. Officials slightly changed the design in 1881.

Wisconsin's motto, "Forward," appears at the top of the state seal. The motto means that Wisconsinites work for progress and change.

Several images on the seal stand for important features in Wisconsin. The badger is the state animal. A sailor represents people who work on Wisconsin's rivers and lakes. A miner stands for the state's mining business. Lead bars and a horn filled with fruit represent Wisconsin's natural resources.

The 13 stars on the bottom of the seal stand for the first 13 states.

State Capitol and Flag

Madison is Wisconsin's capital city. The state capitol building is in Madison. Government officials meet in the capitol to make state laws.

Wisconsin has had three capitol buildings. Workers built the first capitol in 1838. In 1863, workers built a larger building. This capitol burned down in 1904. Workers built the current capitol from 1906 to 1917.

The capitol sits on a hill that overlooks the city. The capitol is built in the shape of an X. The building looks almost the same from all sides. The building is made of granite and marble.

Wisconsin's flag flies over the capitol. The flag is blue with the state's coat of arms in the center. A coat of arms stands for a family, a city, or a state. Wisconsin's coat of arms shows the state seal.

Wisconsin has the only state capitol with a granite dome.

State Bird

The American robin is Wisconsin's state bird. Schoolchildren chose this bird in 1927. The government made the choice official in 1949.

Adult robins are about 9 to 11 inches (23 to 28 centimeters) long. They have dark heads and gray backs. Their breast feathers are red-orange.

Robins are common throughout the United States. Many robins live in Wisconsin in summer. They leave Wisconsin during autumn. Robins spend the winter in the south, where it is warmer. The birds return to Wisconsin in the spring. Many people believe that the robins' return signals the arrival of spring.

Robins build cup-shaped nests out of mud, grass, and twigs. Female robins lay three to five eggs with light blue shells. People call this color "robin's egg blue."

Robins eat berries, insects, and worms.

State Tree

Wisconsin officials wanted to choose a state tree to honor Wisconsin's 100th birthday. The officials asked schoolchildren to vote on a tree. The students chose the sugar maple as the state tree. In 1949, government officials adopted the sugar maple as the state tree.

Sugar maples are medium-sized trees. A fully grown sugar maple can reach more than 100 feet (30 meters) tall. Sugar maple leaves turn bright red in fall.

Wood from sugar maples is heavy and strong. Builders use the valuable wood for furniture and floors. Wooden bowling pins also are made from sugar maple trees.

People harvest sap from sugar maples. People boil the sap to make sweet maple syrup. It takes 40 gallons of maple sap to make one gallon of maple syrup.

Sugar maple trees are tall and strong. Some people call sugar maple trees rock maples.

State Flower

Wisconsin's schoolchildren wanted to choose a state flower. The children voted on Arbor Day in 1909. The wood violet received the most votes. Lawmakers made the schoolchildren's vote official in 1949.

Wood violets are native to Wisconsin. They grow well in dark, shady places such as forests. Thick forests cover large parts of Wisconsin.

Each of these plants grows about 2 to 6 inches (5 to 15 centimeters) tall. The stems and leaves form a circle about 1 foot (30 centimeters) wide.

Wood violets have dark green stems and leaves. Purple blossoms grow on the stems.

Wood violets are perennial plants. They bloom every spring.

State Animal

Wisconsin's official state animal is the badger. People chose the badger because it reminded them of Wisconsin's early miners.

Badgers are small animals. An adult male can be 2 to 3 feet (61 to 91 centimeters) long. It may weigh up to 25 pounds (11 kilograms).

Badgers have short, flat bodies. Badgers are gray with white stripes on their heads and backs. Black markings appear on badgers' heads and faces.

Badgers have several uses for their long, sharp claws. They dig underground burrows for shelter. Badgers use their claws to fight enemies.

Badgers also use their claws to hunt for food. At night, badgers dig into smaller animals' burrows. Badgers eat mice, squirrels, or any other small animals they can catch.

Badgers are fierce animals with sharp teeth.

More State Symbols

State Beverage: In 1986, milk became the official state beverage.

State Dance: The polka became Wisconsin's state dance in 1993. This traditional dance is still popular today.

State Dog: Officials made the American water spaniel the state dog in 1985. This dog is the only breed native to Wisconsin.

State Domestic Animal: Officials named the dairy cow Wisconsin's state domestic animal in 1971. Wisconsin's farms and factories produce many dairy products such as cheese and ice cream. "The Dairy State" is one of Wisconsin's unofficial nicknames.

State Grain: Lawmakers made corn the official state grain in 1991. Wisconsin's farmers grow more corn than farmers in any other state.

State Wildlife Animal: The white-tailed deer became the official state wildlife animal in 1957.

The dairy business is important to Wisconsin. Wisconsin is the nation's leading milk-producing state.

Places to Visit

Indian Burial Mounds at Perrot State Park

Early Native Americans built many burial mounds in Wisconsin. Visitors view some of the mounds in Perrot State Park near Trempaleau. The park sits on top of bluffs that overlook the Mississippi River.

Lambeau Field and the Packer Hall of Fame

The Green Bay Packers play at Lambeau Field. They are the oldest professional football team in the United States. Lambeau Field and the Packer Hall of Fame are in Green Bay.

Old World Wisconsin

Old World Wisconsin is a pioneer village near Eagle. Guides in costumes explain what life was like for early Wisconsin settlers. Visitors see how farmers, carpenters, and bakers worked.

Words to Know

bluff (BLUFF)—a tall, steep bank or cliff
burrow (BUR-oh)—a hole in the ground where an animal lives
coat of arms (KOHT UHV ARMZ)—a drawing usually in the shape of a shield that often has other figures around it; a coat of arms stands for a family, a city, or a state.
perennial (puh-REN-ee-uhl)—a plant that lives and flowers for more than two years
sap (SAP)—a sticky, watery fluid that flows inside trees

Read More

Bratvold, Gretchen. *Wisconsin.* Hello U.S.A. Minneapolis: Lerner Publications, 1997.

Capstone Press Geography Department. *Wisconsin.* One Nation. Mankato, Minn.: Capstone Press, 1997.

Fradin, Dennis Brindell. *Wisconsin.* From Sea to Shining Sea. Chicago: Children's Press, 1992.

Stone, Lynn M. *Dairy Country.* Back Roads. Vero Beach, Fla.: Rourke, 1993.

Thompson, Kathleen. *Wisconsin.* Portrait of America. Austin, Texas: Raintree Steck-Vaughn, 1996.

Useful Addresses

Wisconsin Department of Administration
Capitol Tours
4 East State Capitol
Madison, WI 53702

Wisconsin Department of Tourism
201 West Washington
Madison, WI 53702

Internet Sites

State of Wisconsin
http://www.state.wi.us
Wisconsin Attractions.Roadside America
http://www.roadsideamerica.com/map/wi.html
Wisconsin Department of Tourism
http://tourism.state.wi.us

Index